More by Tracy! ⤵

LEARN WEB APP DEVELOPMENT

Build a web app using Python + Django! Written for non-programmers.

https://hellowebbooks.com/learn-django

LEARN WEB DESIGN

Learn web design fundamentals and shortcuts, aimed at non-designers!

https://hellowebbooks.com/learn-design

ME!
@tracymakes

 SOCIAL MEDIA!

BOOK STUFF!
@hellowebbooks

♡ HELLOWEBBOOKS.com♡

Hey friends!

Are you new to programming? Have you wondered, "Git? What's that?"

(Personally, I grew up in a rural area and "Git" is usually accompanied with "...the heck outta here, you varmint!")

I'm a designer who taught myself how to code and it changed my life. One of the important parts of learning to code was figuring out how to use Git, a version control system for code. Or, in plainer terms, a system to save your coding history so you can back it up, or go back in time to earlier versions, or share with others. It's one of the most useful and most recommended things to learn and use while you're writing programs.

This guide covers the basic commands that you'll be using most of the time. Git itself is a *very* powerful system so we're not going to go into all the advanced things you can do with it (and things you won't need or want to learn until much later).

If you're interested in my other free guides on getting started with programming, check out the Really Friendly Command Line Intro too! Same concept and format as this guide.

Last but not least, this booklet was originally created as an addition to *Hello Web App*, my video course and book teaching beginner web app development using Python and Django. Want to learn how to build a web app, maybe an Instagram clone or your own blog system? Check out Hello Web App: https://hellowebbooks.com/learn-django.

Let's get started!

What's Git?

Say you want to learn to program. You're going to start with Python, Javascript, or another language (doesn't matter which!) and start creating little programs or scripts.

Think of Git as a way to create little waymarkers, or save points, at points in your code's history. When you finish a specific feature, or finish a chapter, you can save the current version of your code. As you check-in your changes, you'll create a log of your history.

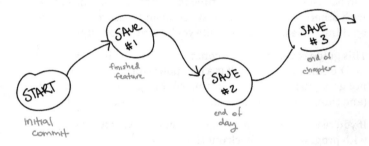

This history is useful for several reasons:

- **You can go back in time!** Say you got everything working with a programming project, so you save your current progress to Git. Then you continue working, and ack—now it doesn't work because there's a bug! You can go back to the last "check-in" of your code and see what changed.

- **You can create branches!** Say your code is working smashingly and you deployed it live. Now you want to work on a new feature that'll take quite a bit of time. Branching allows you *to simultaneously create two different versions* of your code that you can switch between. You can code your new feature on one branch, while keeping your current deployed version of code available in case you need to fix a bug.

- **You can share this history** with something like GitHub, an online hosting service for Git repositories, and be able to view your code and history online. We'll cover this later in the guide!

If that sounds confusing and too abstract, I hear you. It's easier to understand in practice. Let's start!

Let's start playing!

First, we need to install Git. It's easy, I promise you, but for the sake of keeping this guide short, please head over to this very useful guide here for installation: https://git-scm.com/book/en/v2/Getting-Started-Installing-Git

All good?

Let's start things out by creating a project folder and a file within that folder, and we'll use this as our Git playground.

Create a directory and a file in your command line or in your code editor, whichever works best for you.

Initialize Git with git init

Git will only track the projects you tell it to track, so let's tell Git to track this project folder with git init.

Git will create a hidden folder where it'll keep track of things. The only file here that you might touch down the line is the .git/config file, but 99% of the time you don't need to worry about what's going on in the background. But it's useful to know about that directory because if you wanted to remove Git and the history of your project, you can delete that folder.

If this is your very first time using Git, it'll be useful to tell it your preferred username and email. We're going to tell it, with the --global flag, to save this universally on your system so you don't have to tell it these things again later.

Type these into your terminal to set your username and email:

```
git config --global user.name 'YOUR_PREFERRED_USERNAME'
git config --global user.email 'YOUR_EMAIL'
```

See the current status of your project with git status

git status is probably the command you'll be running the most! Type it into your terminal:

```
○○○                      ~~~~~~~~~
~ test $ git status
On branch master
Initial commit
Untracked files:
   (use "git add <file> ..." to include in what will be committed)

  file.txt

Nothing to add to commit but untracked files present (use "git add" to track)
~ test $
```

Git is letting us know that nothing has been committed and that we have one untracked file.

git status will tell you what files are being tracked and whether there are changes made that haven't been "checked-in" yet. Here, we can see that Git is running for this directory, but it isn't currently tracking any files. It wants to be smart and not assume all files in a directory should be tracked, leaving it up to you to tell it what to follow.

Tell Git to track files with git add

We have several different ways to tell Git to track a file:

git add FILENAME
You can explicitly tell it to track current files by specifying the file name.

git add FILENAME FILENAME FILENAME FILENAME
Want to do multiple files in one command? Just list them out!

git add .
Tell Git to add all with a dot

The last command is the command I personally use the most. The dot indicates *all files here* so everything in this directory will be tracked. This is great for something like a Django project, where there will be at least 10 files created and it would be a typing pain to type them all out for Git to track.

We might not want to add *everything* to Git, but we'll worry about that a bit later.

Earlier you created a file in your test directory (*file.txt*) — now, add it to your Git repository (otherwise known as a *repo*):

What about removing files?

The command `git rm FILENAME` will remove the file both from Git *and* from your computer. You're deleting the file.

If you want to just remove the file *from Git* but *keep* the file on your computer, you'll need to pass in the `--cached` flag. So: `git rm --cached FILENAME`.

This isn't something that should be run often at all, but useful to know just in case.

Check status again with git status

Now that we've told Git to track some files, run `git status` again to see what changed. We can see that the file we created earlier is here, and Git is letting us know that it hasn't been saved yet into our Git history.

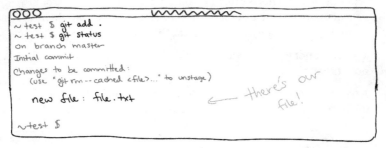

Let's create our first waymarker in our history — our very first commit!

Save your current status with git commit

Let's commit our current status into the Git history, and write a message to go along with it:

```
git commit -a -m "First commit"
```

```
OOO                    ᴍᴍᴍᴍᴍ
~ test $ git commit -a -m "First Commit"
[master (root-commit) dedc415] First commit
 1 file changed, 0 insertions (+), 0 deletions (-)
 create mode 100644 file.txt
~ test $
```

Your numbers might be different but everything else should essentially be the same!

The -m flag tells Git that you want to include a message, which should be done with pretty much every commit. These messages will be included in Git's logs and allows future-you to know why you committed at that moment, like, "Fixed homepage bug related to issue #776." Since this is our very first commit, let's just say that.

Note: *If you don't add a message, Git will open up an editor (using vim by default, which can be confusing to learn). So remember to always add a message when committing, even if it's "WIP" (and if you get stuck in the vim editor, type* :wq *to leave.)*

I also added the -a flag, which is to indicate that you want to commit all files. By default, if you made another change to your file and did another commit, Git would ask you to explicitly add it again (with git add). The -a flag is a shortcut that tells it to go ahead and add all files to the commit *that are already being tracked* by Git. Brand new files will still need to be explicitly added with git add. For me, at this point, I add -a -m "Message" to every commit as a habit since I almost never want to commit without those flags.

Run git status again:

```
OOO                    ᴍᴍᴍᴍᴍ
~ test $ git status
On branch master
nothing to commit, working directory clean
~ test $
```

Voila! Git is telling you everything is normal and nothing has changed since your last commit. Everything is checked in!

You're tracking your files! Now what?

Now that you've started tracking your project files and have made your first commit, you can keep on working. Remember to do a commit every now and again to save your progress when everything is good. Working for a few weeks and checking in a bunch a files at the end with tons of code changes isn't as helpful as committing whenever you achieve a milestone (which could be finishing a small feature, or completing a chapter in a tutorial, or finishing up your work for the day.) This is especially good if you've tied your Git repo in with GitHub or GitLab, as then your work is often backed up at an external source.

I totally understand that it's easy to get wrapped up in programming and forget where you're at or what you've done since your last commit. I personally do this so often! Committing with a less-than-helpful message like "Oh no, haven't committed in a while, I'm working on so-and-so feature" is better than not committing your work at all.

Wait, what changed? See differences with git diff

Remember that `git status` is available at all times to see what files have changed since the last time you've committed. If you haven't committed in a while and notice that, after running `git status`, a file has changes that you don't remember, you can use the command `git diff FILENAME` to see the specific changes in that file.

A lot of gobbledegook! It's comparing the before and after of the file and at the bottom of the output, you can see I added a new line to my file.

If you leave off the filename, `git diff` will show you all the changes across *all* your files. This is a nice way to review your work before making a commit and check it for things that you actually don't want to check in (like debugging statements and whatnot.)

Make another commit, and then check history with git log

Something you probably won't use very often but is still very useful is `git log`. This'll output a list of your commits with their messages and dates so you can see all your history at a glance.

Make a new commit and then run `git log`:

Our two commits so far! Newest is on top.

Nice! To exit this screen, just press "q" to quit. We'll return back here soon.

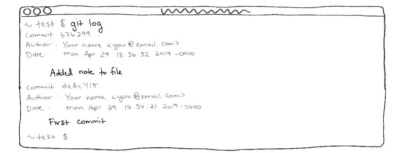

Ack, don't want to commit those changes? Go back to your last checked-in version with git checkout

Say you're working on a feature, and you fall into a rabbit-hole making changes on a file and, at the end, decide that you did the wrong thing and want to start over (I am often guilty of this). Rather than *UNDO*-ing all the way back to your starting point, you can return back to your last committed version of that file with `git checkout FILENAME`.

To see this in action, make some silly changes to a file, and then confirm the changes were made with `git status`. Then run `git checkout` on the file. Tada, you're back to the last checked-in version!

Tada: After checking out our file, it's returned back to the state it was in when it was last committed.

Remember when you ran `git log` and every commit had a ran-

```
~ test $ git status
on branch master
(... rest of output...)

     modified: file.txt
no changes added to commit (use "git add" and/or "git commit -a")
~ test $ git checkout file.txt
~ test $ git status
on branch master
nothing to commit, working directory clean
~ test $
```

dom string assigned to it that looked like `commit 5e4943f93ad-5c242a51c1d6a19d6be5d09c938fd`? You can also use `git checkout COMMITHASH` to go back in time to that commit entirely. This is how you can hop back and forth in time to different states of your code, if you like.

Have files you don't want to track? Set up your .gitignore file

We want to save the history of our code, but there are a lot of other files involved in programming that we don't want to save or share. For example, the plugins we install or files with sensitive information that we don't want to publish on GitHub.

We can list out those files and directories in our *.gitignore* file. These aren't added by Git when we initialize the repository with `git init` — we'll create the file manually and save it in the right place, and Git will automagically read the file and ignore files and directories that match what's in our ignore file.

The name of the file is important (make sure to include the "." at the front of ".gitignore"). It should live next to the hidden .git directory.

To test this out, let's create a dummy file called "ignoreme.txt." First, check that Git sees it with `git status`:

```
~ test $ touch ignoreme.txt
~ test $ git status
on branch master
untracked files:
    (use "git add <file>..." to include in what will be committed)

    ignoreme.txt

nothing added to commit but untracked files present (use "git add")
~ test $
```

Next, create a .gitignore file and put it at the root of your project, where your .git directory is. Within the .gitignore file, put "ignoreme.txt" at the top of the file and save. If we run `git status` again, we can see that the .gitignore file was added, but the *ignoreme.txt file* is no where to be found. Git is successfully ignoring that file!

```
000                    wwwwww
~ test $ touch .gitignore
~ test $ echo "ignoreme.txt" > .gitignore
~ test $ git status
on branch master
untracked files:
    (use "git add <file>... ...)

    .gitignore
nothing added to commit (...)
```

You can also create the file using your text editor if that's easier.

There's a great resource on GitHub that lists out sample *.gitignore* files based on your project type (like Python or JavaScript projects), listing out the typical files that people ignore. You can see and copy the templates here:

https://github.com/github/gitignore

You now know the basics of Git!

The commands we've covered here are the commands that I personally run 95% of the time in all of my projects. To reiterate:

- Initialize Git with `git init`

- Add files to track with `git add` (either everything with `git add .` or individual files with `git add FILENAME`)

- Commit your current progress with `git commit` (adding the `-a` flag to commit all changes and `-m` flag to add a message, so the command is `git commit -a -m "Commit message!"`)

- See the changes with `git diff` (either in one file with `git diff FILENAME` or all changes with just `git diff`)

- Return to the last-checked-in version with `git checkout` (either just one file with `git checkout FILENAME` or return to a previous commit with `git checkout COMMITHASH`, which you would see after running `git log`)

- If you decide you don't want Git to track a file, add it to your `.gitignore` file.

Phew! I promise it'll become second nature with enough practice.

Intermediate Git: Creating branches!

Branching is one of the most useful features of Git. So far, you could imagine your project history as a straight line. Branching allows you to spin off different versions of your project and keep them separate until you want to merge them back together.

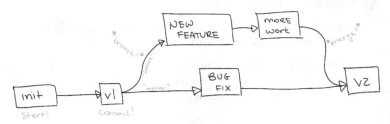

It's easy to see the usefulness if you imagine that your project has gotten to a state where you can launch it live. If you want to code a new feature that would take you a few weeks, you can create a separate branch to contain your changes. You can keep your changes separate from the launched, live, working code, and you can commit changes and make your waypoints within your feature branch over time.

Then, you would have your "master" branch (the default name for your main branch) with your working, deployed code, and your "feature" branch that holds your new feature coding progress. That means if you discover a bug in your deployed code, you can fix it and deploy it without having to also deploy your in-progress feature changes.

When you're ready, Git allows you to merge branches and does it in a fairly smart way. In the previous example, once you've fixed the code in the master branch, you can then run `git merge` to bring those changes into your feature branch. And when you finish your feature branch, you can `git merge` that branch into master and deploy it to your customers.

That's the concept, let's see it in action!

Create a new branch with git checkout -b
BRANCHNAME

Run the command git checkout -b feature in your terminal to create a new branch named "feature".

```
000                   wwwww
~ test $ git checkout -b feature
Switched to a new branch 'feature'
~ test $
```

We'll explore more about git checkout in a second (it's how you'll switch between branches) but adding the -b flag will *create* the branch and switch over to it.

See what branches are available with git branch

If you need to remind yourself what branches you've created, run the command, git branch. I find this particularly useful since I often forget the names of the branches I created.

```
000                   wwwww
~ test $ git branch
* feature
  master
~ test $
```

This is also a handy command to run if you forgot what branch you're currently on! Also, Git will let you know what branch you're on when you run git status:

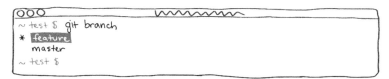

```
000                   wwwww
~ test $ git status          — hey hey!
On branch feature
nothing to commit, working directory clean
~ test $
```

Change what branch you're on with git checkout BRANCHNAME

Now that we can see what branches are available with git branch, we can switch between the two with git checkout BRANCHNAME.

```
~ test $ git checkout master
Switched to branch 'master'
~ test $
```

Stash your changes with git stash and bring them back with git stash pop

Git will whine if you have uncommitted changes in one branch and you try to switch to the other. Git doesn't want to lose your unsaved progress, and doesn't want to assume that this progress should be ported over to the other branch.

If you want to switch branches, you need to save your current progress by either committing it, removing your changes, *or* use something like git stash. This command tells Git to move your changes into an invisible bucket. It's like another dimension (or an unofficial, unlisted branch) that Git will use so you don't lose your progress. The changes will no longer show up when you run git status and this will allow you to move back and forth between branches again.

When you want to bring your changes back, you can use git stash pop. This works on any branch, not just the original branch those changes were on. This is useful if you started working on some changes but realized you were on the wrong branch. Since Git will prevent you from changing branches with uncommitted changes, you can git stash them, change your branch, and then git stash pop to bring them back on the correct branch.

Take your changes from one branch to another with git merge

Finished with the changes on your new branch and want to bring them over to the master branch? We can use git merge to combine the two branches.

To test this out, make some changes on your "feature" branch, then move back to the "master" branch by running the command git checkout master. You can bring *all* the changes you've made to the feature branch over to the master branch with git merge BRANCHNAME (git merge feature if your branch was named "feature")

```
~ test $ git checkout master
Switched to branch 'master'
~ test $ git merge feature
Updating b7296d...c466l8f
Fast-forward
    file.txt | 1+
1 file changed, 1 insertions (+)
~ test $
```

Oh no, there's a conflict!

Git is going to try to be as smart as possible when merging one branch with another, but what happens if things don't merge nicely? If Git doesn't know how to merge in changes (like if there were changes to a piece of code in *both* branches, and it doesn't know if it should keep both changes, or pick one or another), it's going to leave the decision up to you.

When you run git merge it'll let you know if there were any conflicts and will list out the files with those conflicts. In those files, Git will have added >>>>> marks where there is a conflict, and will include *both* versions of the conflicted code, so you can manually pick and choose what to keep and what to lose.

```
000                    mmmmm
~ test $ git merge feature
Auto-merging file.txt
CONFLICT (content): Merge conflict in file.txt
Automatic merge failed; fix conflicts and then commit the result.
~ test $
```

```
000                    mmmmm
<<<<<<< HEAD
This line was changed in master
=======
This line was also changed in feature!
>>>>>>> feature
```

When you look in the file that has the conflict, Git will have added little guides showing the conflicted parts, so you can pick and choose what to keep. After you fix, remember to remove Git's guides as well.

It's nice that Git allows us to fix these issues so we don't accidentally lose any of our hard work when working with branches.

That's cool! So what's GitHub? Or GitLab?

If you've heard of Git, then you've probably heard of GitHub (https://github.com)! Quick overview (as this is mostly beyond the scope of this guide): GitHub can host your project and project history remotely so you have a backup of everything. It would suck to start working on a project and have something happen to your computer and lose your coding work.

This also makes it useful to share your projects with others, as you can "push" to GitHub (make a copy of all your project files on GitHub) and they can "pull" those files onto their own machine.

GitHub also gives you a nicer interface to view your project history, inspect the branches, see what changes were made where, when, and by whom.

If you'd like to use a tool like this (I recommend it), you can use GitHub or its competitor, GitLab (https://gitlab.com). Both give you the option of putting your code in a public or private repository. If you don't care if people can see your code and you don't have any things that you don't want to be public (like secret keys), then a public repo is just fine, but always use a private repo if you have anything you don't want public.

It's fairly easy to link your Git repos with places like GitHub. Check out this great guide for GitHub: https://help.github.com/en/articles/set-up-git.

☆ yay! ☆ We can program with confidence that our work is backed up and history is saved!

There is *so much more* to Git, but this is 99% of what you'll be doing most of the time. It's a very powerful system that's used in a lot of different ways.

In general though, the average person just tracks their project history, commits their progress, and shares that history with a remote repository like GitLab or GitHub. Easy peasy.

I hope this was a fun introduction for you! Feel free to ask any questions you have on the Hello Web App discussion forum: https://discuss.hellowebapp.com

If you're looking for the next step, I invite you to check out Hello Web App, my book and course teaching web app development with Django. Even if you're new to programming and the command line, the book is pretty easy to just follow along, try things out, and learn more by doing. Check it out here: https://hellowebbooks.com/learn-django

Thanks friends, and good luck on your programming journey!

-Tracy

✳ CHEAT SHEET ✳

git init : Initialize Git in your current directory

git status : Output Git's current status

git add : Add files to Git
`git add FILENAME` *or* `git add .`

git rm : Delete files
`git delete FILENAME`

git rm --cached : Remove files from Git
`git rm --cached FILENAME`

git commit : Save your current state
`git commit -a -m "YOUR_MESSAGE"`

git diff : See current changes
`git diff` *or* `git diff FILENAME`

git checkout : *File version:* Return file to last committed state
`git checkout FILENAME`

git checkout -b : Create new branch
`git checkout -b BRANCHNAME`

git branch : See all branches available
`git branch`

git checkout : *Branch version:* Switch branches
`git checkout BRANCHNAME`

git stash : Stash current changes
`git status` *(and* `git stash pop` *to unstash)*

git merge : Merge branch into current branch
`git merge BRANCHNAME`

♡ SAY HI! ♡

@hellowebbooks
↖ twitter/instagram

hellowebbooks.com
↖ website